Study Guide

JONATHAN PARK

The Adventure Begins

Audio Adventure - Volume 1

Table of Contents

Getting the Most From This Study Guide

The Jonathan Park Audio Adventures were produced to help children and families have a strong foundation in which to build their faith! Unfortunately many live as if their belief in the Bible is just another brand of religion. However, God has given us a gift that we often take for granted – He has asked us to believe in truth! Sadly, many Christians are intimidated by evolutionary ideas and told that the Word of God has been disproven by science. The truth is that if God really created the universe, animals, and mankind like He said in Genesis, we should be able to investigate this world and find evidence that what He says is true... and we do!

Think about the difference between the Christian and evolutionary worldviews. If evolution is true, then there is no God and we are the product of random evolutionary processes. As nothing more than a bunch of molecules, we have no purpose in life. On the other hand, if we were created, it means that we were made especially by a loving Creator who has a unique purpose for each of our lives! This difference can completely change a person's life! Truly knowing that God's Word is true is a foundation that will change every aspect of a child's life. That's what we hope to accomplish with the Jonathan Park project – to teach families about scientific evidence that is in harmony with God's Word.

We've designed the audio adventures so families can enjoy them in their cars – while on trips or just running errands. They can listen at home or during family devotional time. Our goal is to provide exciting adventures that run deep with creation apologetics and Biblical lessons. We hope that you enjoy them regardless of where you listen to them!

This Jonathan Park Study Guide has been designed to maximize teaching from each episode in the Jonathan Park Series. Our hope is that after listening to each Jonathan Park Audio Adventure, parents will sit down with their children and work through the information provided in this booklet. Here's how we recommend you use this guide with your child:

1. Listen to an episode from the Jonathan Park: The Adventure Begins – Album #1.
2. Begin your study by praying with your child. Pray that God will teach you truth and continue to build your faith.
3. In the Table of Contents, we've listed Scripture references for each episode. Spend time reading through this section of God's Word.
4. Next, open this Study Guide to the corresponding section. The information is arranged in bite-

sized nuggets – each builds upon the previous one. Read through the information with your child and relate it back to the Word of God.

5. Let the child ask questions, and help them find answers. This Study Guide may be the key to unlocking doubts that a child has. Always follow up a child's question. Refer to other creation science resources, or make a commitment to search for the answer together. These questions are excellent ways to take them deeper into God's Word.

6. End in prayer. Thank the Lord for the specific things He has taught during this time.

"But sanctify the Lord God in your hearts: and be ready always to give an answer to every man that asketh you a reason of the hope that is in you with meekness and fear."

- I Peter 3:15

Do all animal bones become fossils?

It takes very special conditions for bones to be buried fast enough to allow fossilization. Let's find out why...

Imagine this dinosaur dies and falls to the ground. What will happen to his bones? They will either be eaten by other animals or begin to decay from exposure to oxygen and bacteria. These active destroyers will keep those bones from ever having a chance to become fossilized. If decay happens all the time, then why do we find any fossilized bones at all?

When lots of mud and water bury animals very quickly – and if the mud-water mixture contains just the right cementing agent – the bones could begin to fossilize. The minerals in the mixture then replace the minerals in the decaying bones. Eventually, only rocks, in the perfect shape of the bones, will be left!

How could this happen?

Think about this mystery. To make a fossil, an animal must be buried fast and deep, beneath lots of mud and water. How many tons of mud and water would it take to bury hundreds or thousands of dinosaurs so fast that their bones would have a chance to fossilize? Fossilization, on that large a scale, is an awesome event that doesn't happen very often!

There are (2) ways to explain most of the fossils we find...

Evolution Theory	Creation Idea
Millions of freak accidents over millions of years have made the millions of fossils we find.	One huge water catastrophe killed millions of animals at the same time and buried them in mud.

Fossil Bones Graveyard Recipe

Ingredients

- Hundreds of Animals
- Lots of Water
- Lots of Mud
- Cementing Agent

Prepare

Mix the mud, water, and cementing agent. Pour quickly over the animals until all are completely covered by a thick layer of mud.

Wait (but not too long)

Minerals from the surrounding mud sediments will begin to replace the chemicals in some of the bones.

Remove

After the minerals in the mud have replaced the bone, your fossils are finished. The fossilized bones are now rocks that retain the shape of the original bones!

Ghost Ranch

All Around the World are Massive Quarries of Fossilized Dinosaur Remains Called Graveyards.

Ghost Ranch is located about 60 miles north of Santa Fe, New Mexico. The ranch is a conference center owned by the Presbyterian Church. There's also a museum of paleontology, a live animal museum, and a dinosaur quarry. It is truly a fascinating place!

Most exciting is the dinosaur quarry! Paleontologists (scientists who study fossils) have found over a thousand dinosaur fossils. They think there are thousands more still buried there at the ranch. Although they've found the fossil remains of several different dinosaur species (some may not even be named yet), most of the fossils come from Coelophysis (SEE-low-FIE-sis). A Coelophysis dinosaur was about nine feet long and slender, with hollow bones.

What Killed the Dinosaurs at Ghost Ranch?

**Like many other dinosaur graveyards,
Ghost Ranch tells the story of a huge, catastrophic flood!**

Dr. Edwin R. Colbert – *The Scientist behind Ghost Ranch*

It wasn't until 1947 that a young paleontologist, Edwin R. Colbert, heading for fieldwork in the petrified forest of Arizona, made a sightseeing trip to Ghost Ranch with two colleagues. Dr. Colbert had been intrigued with Ghost Ranch ever since studying fossil remains uncovered there three years before. During their 1947 trip, the three men literally stumbled upon the discovery of one of the largest concentrations of dinosaur deposits ever recorded.

After removing 13 blocks weighing up to four tons each, the 1947-48 excavation season came to a close. The quarry was then abandoned for 32 years until 1981-82, when once again Dr. Colbert was asked to supervise the removal of more Coelophysis from Ghost Ranch. This time 16 blocks weighing six to ten tons each were transported to various museums around the country.

Which idea fits the facts better – evolution or creation? If evolution were true, we should see many animals fossilized, one at a time or in small groups, due to localized disasters. However, if a worldwide flood really happened as in the days of Noah, we should find all around the globe evidence of massive destruction and gigantic fossil deposits caused by the world-wide flood. What do we find? Throughout the world we find massive dinosaur deposits containing thousands of dinosaurs – buried quickly by a huge water catastrophe, and fossilized into giant dinosaur graveyards! One excellent example is Ghost Ranch in northern New Mexico.

Ghost Ranch Observations

Paleontologists think that streams, which periodically overflowed their banks, deposited the mud surrounding the dinosaur fossils.

These sediments contain evidence that deposits were cut away and then refilled by water currents.

The fossils show no signs of exposure or decay, which indicates a quick burial.

The bones lie in a jumbled mess. It looks as if many of the fossils were first deposited and then picked up again by water and moved somewhere else.

Their necks of many of the skeletons were bent unnaturally backward over their backs.

The bones do not show evidence that the dinosaurs trampled one another, which may also indicate a quick burial.

Many of the fossils appear to have been transported by large amounts of water after their death.

Some of the skeletons face in the same direction, suggesting that they were carried into position by water currents.

Is Ghost Ranch Evidence for a Worldwide Flood?

Thousands of dinosaur fossils lie buried together in massive heaps – most in huge, jumbled piles. In fact, the evidence seems to show that the dinosaurs were first buried, only to be ripped out of the ground and redeposited somewhere else.

Dr. Edwin Colbert's work confirms that a water catastrophe killed these dinosaurs. He claims that such a catastrophe is the best explanation for the evidence that he and others have discovered over the last 50 years.

If a worldwide flood, like Noah's flood, really did occur, isn't this the type of evidence creationists would expect to find? The Bible tells us that all land – dwelling animals that did not go on Noah's ark were killed by the flood waters.

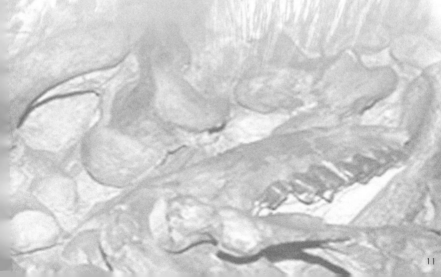

Other Dinosaur Quarries

Ghost Ranch isn't the only dinosaur graveyard – they're found all over the world! In the United States there are other quarries in Montana, Wyoming, Utah, Colorado, and Arizona. These huge dinosaur deposits are a testimony to a catastrophic worldwide flood!

San Juan Basin, *Farmington, New Mexico*
A mix of dinosaurs were found buried at this site. They include Parasaurolophus, Kritosaurus, Pentaceratops, Albertosaurus, and Alamosaurus dinosaurs. Evolutionists claim that these dinosaurs lived in a river flood plain and that there was a seacoast nearby.

Kirland Formation, *San Juan Basin, New Mexico*
Many partial skeletons and skulls buried in a jumbled mess, deposited in mudstone.

Ghost Ranch, *Abiquiu, New Mexico*
One thousand Coelophysis dinosaur fossils have been unearthed from this quarry. Paleontologists think there may be another 9,000 left! Evolutionists working at this site claim that flooding from a river drowned all these creatures.

COLORADO

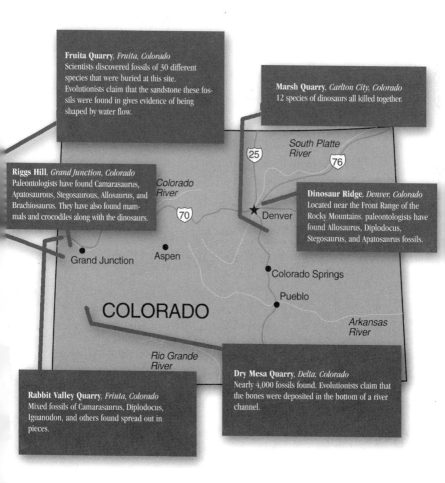

Fruita Quarry, *Fruita, Colorado*
Scientists discovered fossils of 30 different species that were buried at this site. Evolutionists claim that the sandstone these fossils were found in gives evidence of being shaped by water flow.

Marsh Quarry, *Carlton City, Colorado*
12 species of dinosaurs all killed together.

Riggs Hill, *Grand Junction, Colorado*
Paleontologists have found Camarasaurus, Apatosaurous, Stegosaurous, Allosaurus, and Brachiosaurus. They have also found mammals and crocodiles along with the dinosaurs.

Dinosaur Ridge, *Denver, Colorado*
Located near the Front Range of the Rocky Mountains. paleontologists have found Allosaurus, Diplodocus, Stegosaurus, and Apatosaurus fossils.

Dry Mesa Quarry, *Delta, Colorado*
Nearly 4,000 fossils found. Evolutionists claim that the bones were deposited in the bottom of a river channel.

Rabbit Valley Quarry, *Fruita, Colorado*
Mixed fossils of Camarasaurus, Diplodocus, Iguanodon, and others found spread out in pieces.

South Platte River

Colorado River

Denver

Aspen

Grand Junction

Colorado Springs

Pueblo

COLORADO

Arkansas River

Rio Grande River

ARIZONA

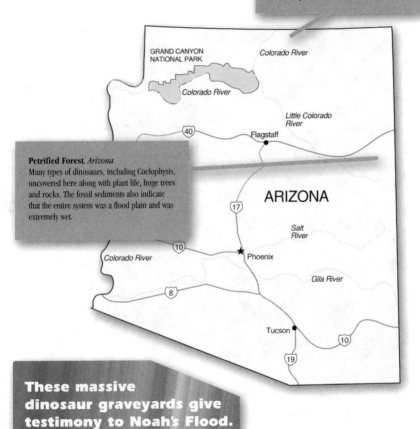

Moenave Formation, *Page, Arizona*
They've found partial skeletons of fish, turtles, and Theropod dinosaurs.

GRAND CANYON NATIONAL PARK

Colorado River

Colorado River

Little Colorado River

(40) Flagstaff

Petrified Forest, *Arizona*
Many types of dinosaurs, including Coelophysis, uncovered here along with plant life, huge trees and rocks. The fossil sediments also indicate that the entire system was a flood plain and was extremely wet.

ARIZONA

(17)

Salt River

(10)
Colorado River

★ Phoenix

Gila River

(8)

Tucson

(10)

(19)

These massive dinosaur graveyards give testimony to Noah's Flood.

Warm Spring Ranch, *Thermopolis, Wyoming*
So far, scientists have pulled 1,000 fossils from this site. They are Camarasaur, Diplodocus, Apatosaur, Stegosaur, Allosaur, and possibly Camptosaur and Carnosaur groups.

• Sheridan

YELLOWSTONE
NATIONAL PARK

Yellowstone
River

GRAND TETON
NATIONAL PARK

Snake
River

Bighorn
River

Powder
River

{26}

Howe Quarry, *Shell, Wyoming*
More than 4,000 bones were uncovered here, mostly Barosaurus, Camarasaurus, Diplodocus, and Apatosaurus. Skin impressions also found. Fossils found in a thick sandstone layer.

Lance Creek Formation, *Laranze, Wyoming*
They've found Edmontosaurus, Tyrannosaurus Rex, hundreds of Triceratops, and several other types of dinosaurs all buried together in what evolutionists claim was a coastal flood plain. They also found fish, frogs, salamanders, crocodiles, mammals, and birds.

Casper

WYOMING

Como Bluff Dinosaur Quarry, *Medicine Bow, Wyoming*
Since 1877, thousands of vertebrate fossils have been recovered from more than 14 different species of dinosaurs. Fossils from lungfishes, frogs, salamander, turtles, and crocodiles have also been found. Evolutionists claim that these fossils were deposited on an ancient flood plain.

Laramie • ★ Cheyenne

Bone Cabin Quarry, *Laramie, Wyoming*
Fifty partial dinosaur skeletons buried together including Diplodocus, Camarasaurus, Apatosaurus, Orantholestes, Camptosaurus, Dryosaurus, and Stegosaurus.

WYOMING

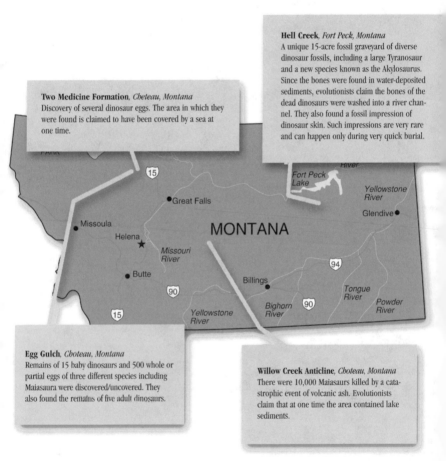

Hell Creek, *Fort Peck, Montana*
A unique 15-acre fossil graveyard of diverse dinosaur fossils, including a large Tyranosaur and a new species known as the Akylosaurus. Since the bones were found in water-deposited sediments, evolutionists claim the bones of the dead dinosaurs were washed into a river channel. They also found a fossil impression of dinosaur skin. Such impressions are very rare and can happen only during very quick burial.

Two Medicine Formation, *Cheteau, Montana*
Discovery of several dinosaur eggs. The area in which they were found is claimed to have been covered by a sea at one time.

Egg Gulch, *Choteau, Montana*
Remains of 15 baby dinosaurs and 500 whole or partial eggs of three different species including Maiasaura were discovered/uncovered. They also found the remains of five adult dinosaurs.

Willow Creek Anticline, *Choteau, Montana*
There were 10,000 Maiasaurs killed by a catastrophic event of volcanic ash. Evolutionists claim that at one time the area contained lake sediments.

Dinosaur National Monument

Dinosaur National Monument in Utah is another large dinosaur quarry. At this site, they've found over 1,600 dinosaur fossils! However, dinosaurs aren't the most common fossils found there – clams are! What better evidence for the worldwide flood could there be than tons of clams mixed in with dinosaur fossils that were buried quickly by mud?

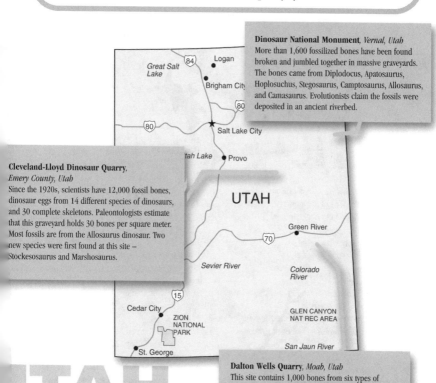

Dinosaur National Monument, *Vernal, Utah*
More than 1,600 fossilized bones have been found broken and jumbled together in massive graveyards. The bones came from Diplodocus, Apatosaurus, Hoplosuchus, Stegosaurus, Camptosaurus, Allosaurus, and Camasaurus. Evolutionists claim the fossils were deposited in an ancient riverbed.

Cleveland-Lloyd Dinosaur Quarry,
Emery County, Utah
Since the 1920s, scientists have 12,000 fossil bones, dinosaur eggs from 14 different species of dinosaurs, and 30 complete skeletons. Paleontologists estimate that this graveyard holds 30 bones per square meter. Most fossils are from the Allosaurus dinosaur. Two new species were first found at this site – Stockesosaurus and Marshosaurus.

Dalton Wells Quarry, *Moab, Utah*
This site contains 1,000 bones from six types of dinosaurs. The bones rest in a layer of limey mudstone.

17

Massive Layers

In *Jonathan Park and the Secret of the Hidden Cave*, the Park and Brenan families find a fictitious cave carved in a layer of rock known as limestone.

Lime usually comes from the ocean, yet scientists find huge deposits of this rock on every continent – hundreds of miles away from the sea.

Across

1. The huge event that killed most land animals, and made millions of fossils *(two words)*.
4. Dinosaur parts that become fossilized.
7. The place where tons of Coelophysis dinosaur fossils are buried under huge amounts of hardened mud layers *(two words)*.
8. Dinosaurs are often thought of as a _____ of reptile.
9. Where dinosaurs' fossils are put on display for people to see.
10. Creatures in legends. Many think these might have been actual dinosaurs.
12. When an entire group of animals die. For example, most dinosaurs probably died during the flood. Those which survived might have gone _____ not long after the flood because the world had changed so much.
17. This great water-dwelling creature is described in the Bible in Job, Chapter 41.
18. A great creature, which has gone extinct.

Down

1. During Noah's Flood it rained both day and _____.
2. Bones become _____ when covered quickly and nearby minerals replace the bone material.
3. Evolutionists want to believe that dinosaur fossils are very _____.
4. In Job 40:15, the Bible tells us about a great creature which might have been a dinosaur. The _____'s tail was as big as a cedar tree.
5. The bone part of a dinosaur's head.
6. To form fossils, you need lots of _____, mud, and the right cementing agents.
7. Book of the Bible that tells us about God creating all creatures, including dinosaurs.
11. The Bible tells us that God created land animals including dinosaurs on the _____ day of the creation week.
13. God is the _____ of dinosaurs and all living creatures.
14. The average size of a dinosaur was about the size of a small horse. Some were very short; others were very _____.
15. Scientists who study fossils are called paleontologists. They use tools to _____ up dinosaurs.
16. We learn the truth about dinosaurs from God's Word, which is called the _____.

Creation scientists believe the flood picked up this limey mud from the very bottom of the ocean and deposited it around the world where it hardened into limestone.

There is also another layer of rock known as the Chinle Formation, which stretches throughout northern Utah, southern Nevada, and Colorado. The fact that the Chinle Formation covers such large areas provides excellent evidence for Noah's Flood. Thousands of dinosaurs have been buried in this layer – including the ones at Ghost Ranch!

In the beginning, God created Adam and Eve with the ability to speak, and to think...

...but not everyone believes that.

EVOLUTION

Evolution says that we started out as a single-celled organism, and that we've been evolving for millions and millions of years. According to evolution, our closest ancestor is an ape-like creature.

If evolution is true, then mankind started out very dumb – we couldn't speak or think intelligent thoughts. The first humans wouldn't have known how to make fire much less build cities, or play musical instruments, or work with metal. Early civilizations would have been very primitive.

So what does science say?

Archaeologists are finding new evidence that early mankind was intelligent!

Over the last decade alone, scientists have discovered site after site that shows the intellectual abilities of past societies. Ancient man had the ability to farm, play instruments, form governments, practice religion, and manufacture tools and weapons.

Because of these discoveries, evolutionists have continually pushed back their timeline for the evolution of "civilized" man. Did man evolve earlier, or is there a better explanation?

The Mayans studied Astronomy and had a simple understanding of movements in our galaxy.

The Ancient Incas built complex stone structures that boggle the imagination. Only recently does modern man possess the technology to accomplish such feats.

Out Of Place ArtifactS

OOPARTS is an acronym for "out of place artifacts." These tools, pottery, or weapons are items that have been left behind by older civilizations. They are considered "out of place" because they seem too sophisticated for the time period in which they are found — according to the evolutionary time frame.

One example of an OopArt is an iron bowl found in coal bed that evolutionists say formed millions of years ago, long before man had the ability to work with metal. Such artifacts raise questions about the evolutionary story.

Did man evolve earlier than thought, or was he created smart from the start?

The evidence we find fits what the Bible tells us!

CREATION

The Bible says that God created people on Day 6 of creation week. Right from the very start Adam and Eve could talk and think intelligently – they didn't evolve from an ape-like creature!

News Release

A depiction of Tell Hamoukar

May 2000 - Syria

A team of archaeologists has uncovered the remains of a large civilization in Sy known as Tell Hamoukar.

This new discovery is challenging th evolutionary timeline for the civiliza tion of man.

McGuire Gibson, the co-director the Tell Hamoukar site, has been quoted as saying, "We need to reconsider our ideas about the beginnings of civilization, push time further back."

Tell Hamoukar is just one of several recent finds showing the early intelligence of ancient man!

Genesis 4:20 - 22, "And Adah bare Jabal: he was the father of such as dwell in tents, and of such as have cattle. And his brother's name was Jubal: he was the father of all such as handle the harp and organ. And Zillah, she also bare Tubalcain, an instructor of every artificer in brass and iron: and the sister of Tubalcain was Naamah."

The people in Genesis made tents, raised cattle, played musical instruments, and trained others how to build things from brass and iron. They had a sophisticated civilization, right from the start.

Does it matter?

If we evolved, it means we somehow came about through random chance accidents and have no real purpose in life. This means that mankind started off stupid and evolved to where we are now.

However, the Bible tells us that each one of us was created unique, with a special purpose!

Genesis 1:27, "So God created man in his own image, in the image of God created he him; male and female created he them."

Genesis tells us that God sent a worldwide flood to destroy the wicked people that lived during that time. Only Noah and his family survived on the Ark.

Genesis
Chapter Seven

11 *In the six hundredth year of Noah's life, in the second month, the seventeenth day of the month, the same day were all **the fountains of the great deep** broken up, and the windows of heaven were opened.*
12 *And the rain was upon the earth forty days and forty nights.*

In Genesis 7:11, the Bible mentions the "fountains of the great deep." Creation scientists believe that the Bible is referring to underwater volcanic activity.

As the super hot magma from these fountains met with the cold ocean water, they would have formed huge steam plumes that would rise to the surface, and release great amounts of water into the atmosphere. It's possible that this process could provide enough water to cause rain for forty days and forty nights, just as the Bible says.

As a result of the volcanic activity and catastrophic effects of the Flood, the ocean temperature would have been warmer after the Flood.

Scientists have drilled long columns of material from the ocean floor. Inside these cores, scientists find the fossil remains of skeletons from ocean-dwelling animals.

By comparing the ratio of Oxygen-18 ($^{18}_{8}O$) to the amount of Oxygen-16 ($^{16}_{8}O$) molecules in these fossils, scientists can determine the temperature of the ocean represented by that section of the column.

Using this information, and the creation timeline, creation scientists can chart the past temperature history of the oceans.

This graph shows the temperatures of the earth's oceans for 1,600 years after the Flood (based on the creation understanding of the age of the earth). These temperatures are based on temperatures calculated from the oxygen ratios in fossils found in sea floor cores.

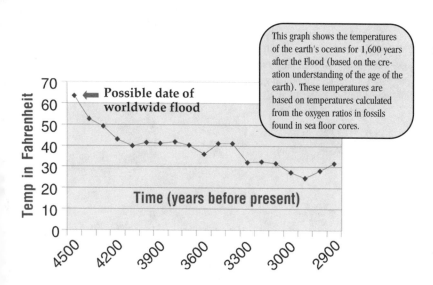

Notice the warmer ocean temperatures at the time of the worldwide flood. This was probably due to the volcanic activity and other catastrophic processes that were part of the Flood.

The theory that the oceans were warmer immediately following the Flood seems to be confirmed by the oxygen ratios in the layers of ocean fossils!

Creation scientists may have a better explanation for what started the ice age than evolutionists!

Creation scientists wanted to know how warmer ocean temperatures would affect the world's climate. Using a computer and the Community Climate Model software (developed at the National Center for Atmospheric Research), scientists plugged in their new information about the high temperatures of the ocean.

The computer model showed that warmer water would create a much higher rate of evaporation. More water in the atmosphere would lead to higher rates of snowfall near the earth's poles. The computer model showed the world would have experienced an ice age not too long after Noah's Flood!

Evolutionists believe that the earth is billions of years old. They interpret the same data that creation scientists use but expand it to millions of years instead of just a few thousand. They believe there were several ice ages over hundreds of thousands of years. However, they don't really have a good explanation for what caused these ice ages.

With this new model for the ice age, creation scientists do have an explanation for what started the ice age – a worldwide flood. It looks like creation scientists now have a much better explanation for the ice age than do evolutionists!

One of the main criticisms with creation scientists' ice age theory is the rapid formation of ice. Evolutionists say it would take much longer to form ice sheets than creationists predict. For example, they say that the Greenland ice sheets have to be 160,000 years old.

However, some P-38 aircraft crashed on the Greenland ice pack during Word War II. Over the last fifty or so years, those airplanes have been covered by 250 feet of ice. If we measure how fast the ice pack grew, and take into consideration other important factors, we could calculate the age of the Greenland ice pack to be less than 1,000 years old.

As a matter of fact, as a result of warmer oceans after the Flood, climate models show that two miles of ice could accumulate in less than 500 years! Instead of many long ice ages, there may have been one ice age that happened quickly as a result of a worldwide flood.

Not long after the Flood, God divided the people!

The Tower of Babel was after the Flood, possibly as the ice age began.

In Genesis Chapter 11, the Bible tells us that mankind again became evil. To rebel against God man decided to unite and build a tower to show man's glory. At the time, everyone spoke the same language. However, God decided to stop their evil plans. The Bible says that He caused the people to begin speaking different languages and scattered them over the face of the earth.

It would make sense to assume that people speaking the same language would stick together. These language groups probably moved to find their own place in the world and became isolated from other groups.

Because of this isolation, these people groups had children that took on the traits of their specialized group. Soon, the different people groups and tribes had their own very distinct traits. This seems to be the Biblical explanation for where the different ethnic groups and traditions came from!

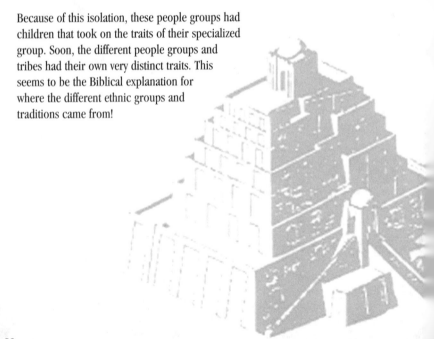

Not long after the Tower of Babel, different people groups scattered around the world. Many scientists believe that at this time a group of people crossed from Russia to Alaska. There are several theories on how this might have happened. Some believe they came by boat; others believe they came by a land or ice bridge.

Because of the artifacts being found at paleoindian sites in Florida, some scientists now believe that these people traveled across the United States to Florida before spreading throughout the rest of the continent.

The Aucilla River is just below Tallahassee. This river has been a site in which many paleoindian artifacts have been discovered. Arrowheads, spearheads, drills made from rock, and many other artifacts have been found. One of the most exciting discoveries was a mastodon tusk with carvings! This tusk may have been one of the earliest pieces of artwork found on American soil!

Being available to serve the Creator

In his latest adventure, Jonathan Park learned a new lesson about serving the Lord. Sometimes we don't feel like doing what God wants, but we don't know what He has in store for us. Living for the Creator every day is the most important thing that we can do. I guess Grandpa Benjamin summed it up when he read...

"Therefore, my beloved brethren, be ye steadfast, unmoveable, always abounding in the work of the Lord, forasmuch as ye know that your labour is not in vain in the Lord."
- I Corinthians 15:58

There's also another important verse about being available to God...

"I beseech you therefore, brethren, by the mercies of God, that ye present your bodies a living sacrifice, holy, acceptable unto God, which is your reasonable service." - Romans 12:1

Are you willing to be available to do what God calls you to do? Why don't you pray and let Him know you're ready to live for Him!

Created Equal

Because we're all descendants from the groups separated at the Tower of Babel, we can never say that one group is better than another. We all came from the same place. We're created equal – in God's image!

Activity: Divide a box of crayons into four equal groups. Color the two people in set A with one group of crayons, then color the two people in set B with the second group of crayons, and so on.

After coloring the pictures to your left, compare the four different groups. Ask the follow questions:

1. Do the two people in set A look similar to each other?
2. Do the two people in set A look a little different from the people in set D?
3. Why do the people in the same set look similar yet a little different from the other sets?

The different colors represent traits that were present at the Tower of Babel. Everyone was at Babel, so all of the human traits were represented there. When the people broke off into smaller groups, only a partial set of traits went with each group – just like when you colored the pictures with only a fourth of your crayons. Each group of people looked like the traits available in their group.

With people, however, there're more differences than just color. People are different shapes, have different facial features, and different abilities.

Getting into the Scriptures

A devotional for children & parents

1. **Begin with Prayer!**

2. **Look up the Bible verses and fill in the blanks** (Please note that the Scripture references listed are from the King James Version.)

3. **Parents, using the Scriptures in this study, take time to further explain the truths presented in each point.**

---

1 Evolution teaches that living organisms evolved from non-living chemicals into a complex human body over millions of years. But God's Word shows us that man was created by the Creator of life on the sixth day of creation and that he was made "smart from the start."

Genesis 1:26 - "And God said, Let us make man in our _____, after our _____: and let them have _____ over the fish of the sea, and over the fowl of the air, and over the cattle, and over all the earth, and over every creeping thing that creepeth upon the earth."

Note: Scientists who study ancient history of civilization believe that man must have certain characteristics in order to be sophisticated. Due to man's fall into sin from his original state, it is reasonable to believe that man from Adam to Noah possessed numerous characteristics that are no longer common in any single culture since the time of Noah.

Genesis 4:17 - "And Cain knew his wife; and she conceived, and bare Enoch: and he _____ a _____, and called the name of the city, after the name of his son, Enoch."

Note: Engineering skills are evident here. In order to plan and develop a city of any size, great knowledge and understanding to plan and build is necessary.

Genesis 4:20-22 - "And Adah bare Jabal: he was the father of such as dwell in _____, and of such as have _____. And his brother's name was Jubal: he was the father of all such as handle the _____ and _____. And Zillah, she also bare Tubal-cain, an _____ of every artificer in brass and iron: and the sister of Tubal-cain was Naamah."

Note: Contrary to evolutionary archaeologists' (scientists who study past civilizations) attempts to organize human history in terms of various supposed "ages" – Stone Age, Bronze Age, Iron Age, etc – the book of Genesis indicates that early men were skilled as tentmakers, herdsmen, musicians, and metal instructors.

Even though God made man with such a wonderful beginning, man still chose to disobey God. In the Bible, disobedience to God is called sin. Romans 5:19 – "For as by one man's disobedience many were made sinners..."

Because man continued to go in the way of sin, God decided to destroy mankind with a flood. But even though God sent a flood to destroy mankind for his sin, He saved a man named Noah, who along with his family, still believed and obeyed God. 2 Peter 2:5 – "And spared not the old world, but saved Noah the eighth person, a preacher of righteousness, bringing in the flood upon the world of the ungodly;"

Gen. 6:17 - "And, behold, I, even I, do bring a flood of waters upon the earth, to destroy all flesh, wherein is the breath of life, from under heaven; and every thing that is in the earth shall die."

Genesis 7:11 - "In the six hundredth year of Noah's life, in the second month, the seventeenth day of the month, the same day were all the _____ of the _____ _____ broken up, and the windows of heaven were opened."

Note: The actual cause of the Flood is identified as the eruption of the waters in the "great deep" and the opening of the "windows of heaven." The fountains of the "great deep" were probably undersea volcanoes releasing hot magma into the cold ocean waters, causing huge steam plumes that erupted into the earth's atmosphere. After the Flood, the oceans were probably much warmer. Using this concept, scientists simulated these conditions in a computer, and the results showed the earth would begin an ice age.

Job 37:9-10 - "Out of the south cometh the whirlwind: and _____ out of the _____. By the breath of God _____ is given: and the breadth of the waters is straitened."

Job 38:29-30 - "Out of whose womb came the _____? and the hoary _____ of heaven, who hath gendered it? The waters are hid as with a stone, and the face of the deep is _____."

Note: Job, a man after which the Book of Job in the Old Testament was named, lived not too long after the Flood. The Book of Job contains many references to cold, snow, ice, and frost that can be better understood in the context of a world that had just recently recovered from the Flood of Noah, followed by the Ice Age. The verses to the left are from the book of Job, which is believed to be the oldest book of the Bible. Job lived before Moses, and probably during the time of Abraham (around 2000 B.C.).

 Even after such a judgment as a worldwide flood, man continued to choose his own way of life and not God's ways. Proverbs 16:25 – "There is a way that seemeth right unto a man, but the end thereof are the ways of death."

Gen. 11:1, 4 - "And the whole earth was of one language, and of one speech...And they said, Go to, let us build us a city and a _____, whose top may reach unto heaven; and let us make us a _____, lest we be _____ abroad upon the face of the whole earth."

Note: God commanded man to be fruitful, multiply, and fill the earth. They rebelled against this request, gathered together, and then to add insult planned to build the tower to further shake their fist at God ...

God's plan to fill and subdue the earth was to be implemented through subdividing and developing mankind into organized communities or nations.

The authority of human government was to prevent and punish individuals or nations for any dishonest or deceitful methods used for personal gain (i.e., Genesis 14 – Battle of the Kings).

Genesis 11:6, 8 - "And the LORD said, Behold, the people is one, and they have all one language; and this they begin to do: and now nothing will be _____ from them, which they have _____ to do...So the LORD scattered them abroad from thence upon the face of all the earth: and they left off to build the city."

Note: This Origin of the Nations resulted in many differences besides language and physical traits. This is because the entire body of genetic (that which is hereditary) information present at the Tower of Babel in Genesis 11 was sorted into each of the isolated groups.

The Tower of Babel illustrates how man would rather get lost in the crowd ("who will notice", "everyone else is doing it", "strength in numbers", "united we stand, divided we fall", "misery loves company") rather than take individual responsibility. Mankind chooses to rebel against God's ways in order to become unified. God's children are called to be a "peculiar people" (1 Pet. 2:9), different from the majority who are set on their own way of life. (Matthew 7:13-14)

In Conclusion:

It is important to realize that true faith in God always involves historical events, not just ethical or moral ones. The Bible is not a book of fairy tales. It is an accurate record of God's truth about where man came from, what sin is, how it has infected all of creation, and how God is going to one day restore His creation from the curse He place upon it due to man's rebellion.

Many of the greatest scientists of the past believed in creation!

These are only a few examples...

Robert Boyle 1627-1691

Robert Boyle was the father of modern chemistry. He discovered the scientific laws that show the relationship of gas pressures to temperature and volume. He is also considered to be the greatest physical scientist of his time.

He spent much of his time studying God's Word and invested his own money to support Bible translation. He also sponsored a series of talks known as the "Boyle Lectures" that taught Christians about the facts for their faith.

Isaac Newton is most famous for the discovery of gravity, but he also formulated the three laws of universal motion and helped to develop the math known as calculus. His work laid the foundation for the great scientific law of energy conservation, and he developed the particle theory of light propagation. As an astronomer, he made the first reflecting telescope.

Isaac Newton 1642-1727

Newton, a believer in the Creator, wrote papers defending creation and the Bible. He believed that the worldwide flood, as described in Genesis, accounted for most of earth's features. He also believed in the six-day creation account found in Genesis.

Newton said, "This most beautiful system of the sun, planets, and comets could only proceed from the counsel and dominion of an intelligent and powerful Being."

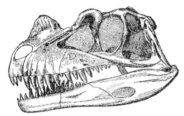

John Woodward lived from 1665 - 1728 and was one of the first paleontologists – scientists who study fossils. He believed the fossil record showed great evidence for the worldwide flood of the Bible.

Samuel F. B. Morse is best known for his invention of the telegraph. He also designed the first camera in America.

Morse once wrote, *"The nearer I approach to the end of my pilgrimage, the clearer is the evidence of the divine origin of the Bible, the grandeur and sublimity of God's remedy for fallen man are more appreciated, and the future is illuminated with hope and joy."*

Samuel F.B. Morse
1791-1872

Wernher von Braun
1912-1977

Wernher von Braun was one of the world's top rocket scientists. He was Germany's top rocket engineer before moving to America. He designed the V-2 rocket, which placed man on the moon. He also served as the Director at NASA's Marshall Space Flight Center.

Not only was von Braun the world's top rocket scientist, but he was also a committed creationist. He once said, *"Manned space flight is an amazing achievement, but it has opened for mankind thus far only a tiny door for viewing the awesome reaches of space. An outlook through this peephole at the vast mysteries of the universe should only confirm our belief in the certainty of its Creator."*

Creation Science

What do milk and creation science have in common?

The answer is...
Louis Pasteur
1822 - 1894

Louis Pasteur, physicist and chemist, made one of the most significant contributions in medicine – he established the germ theory of disease. He also identified several harmful bacteria and made vaccines to cure many diseases like rabies, diphtheria, anthrax, and others. Many people owe their lives to the work of Pasteur.

It was also the work of Pasteur that led to the process of pasteurization. This process of heating milk to a specific temperature for a period of time makes milk safe for human consumption by destroying all bacteria that may be harmful.

People used to believe that mice could form from dirty rags, or that if you left out rotting meat, maggots would come to life. This idea is known as spontaneous generation – that life can form from non-living objects.

Today, long after Pasteur, evolutionists believe in a different form of spontaneous generation. They teach that a big bang created all matter in the universe, and then random chance accidents combined this dead matter and chemicals into living cells. Evolutionary theory states life had to come from non-living objects.

In Pasteur's most famous experiment, he disproved spontaneous generation. First he took some broth and then boiled it to kill any microbes living inside the broth. Then he placed the broth in special glassware that allowed air to penetrate the broth but kept microbes out. Sure enough, no microbes formed out of the broth. This proved that living microbes could only come from other microbes – they didn't form from the non-living broth. This experiment proved once and for all that living things can only come from living things. Yet, evolutionists still believe that somewhere, somehow, the first life came from non-living matter!

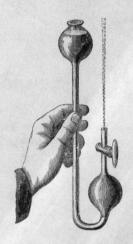

Thousands of Scientists living today believe in the Creator.

Like the ones heard on **Jonathan Park and the Disaster at Brenan Bluff...**

Dr. Russ Humphreys served for many years as a geophysicist at Sandia National Laboratories. He wrote a book on the origin of the universe titled, *Starlight and Time* and is also working with a team of scientists known as R.A.T.E. to demonstrate that radioisotope dating does not prove the earth to be millions of years old. He recently joined the staff of the Institute for Creation Research.

Dr. John Baumgardner, a geophysicist at Los Alamos National Laboratories, is also part of the R.A.T.E. team. He designed the computer program that is used by scientists all over the world to understand the way in which the earth's surface plates move. He has been studying the effect that a worldwide flood would have on the earth.

Dr. Danny Faulkner is a professor of physics and astronomy at the University of South Carolina, at Lancaster. His research has brought him to the conclusion that the Big-Bang theory is wrong and that the evidence instead points to a Creator.

Dr. Otto Berg was an astrophysicist for NASA from its beginnings. During his time at NASA, he saw more and more evidence that convinced him that God made the universe.

Dr. John Morris is a geology professor and President of the Institute for Creation Research. He has explored Mount Ararat over ten times in search of Noah's Ark. His goal is to show that true science points to our Creator.

Dr. Donald DeYoung is a professor of physics and astronomy at Grace College in Winona Lake, Indiana. He studied the relationship of the moon and the earth and has shown how God designed them both. He's also a member of the R.A.T.E. team.

Dr. Ken Cumming, who received a Ph.D. in biology and ecology from Harvard University, now serves as the Dean of ICR's Graduate School. Much of his research has shown the impossibility of biological evolution.

Dr. Karen Jensen has her degree in biology, with an emphasis in paleobotany. She now operates a nature center called "Leoni Meadows Nature Center" in Sacramento and teaches her visitors about evidence for the Creator.

Dave Phillipps, a professor at The Master's College in Santa Clarita, California, is currently working on his Ph.D. in anthropaleontology. Mr. Phillipps studies the fossil record and has been fascinated by dinosaur graveyards. He has pointed out that these fossil graveyards are great evidence for a worldwide flood.

Did God always exist?
The Bible Says...

Before the mountains were brought forth, or ever thou hadst formed the earth and the world, even from everlasting to everlasting, thou art God. Psalm 90:2

Blessed be the LORD God of Israel from everlasting to everlasting: and let all the people say, Amen. Praise ye the LORD. Psalm 106:48

I am Alpha and Omega, the beginning and the end, the first and the last. Revelation 22:13

For by him were all things created, that are in heaven, and that are in earth, visible and invisible, whether they be thrones, or dominions, or principalities, or powers: all things were created by him, and for him: And he is before all things, and by him all things consist. Colossians 1:16-17

Think about it

Without God, how did life originate? Matter (what a thing is made of) needs a beginning. Evolutionists don't like the idea of a Creator because such an idea requires faith. However, they're in the same boat! It requires more faith to believe in evolution because everything needs a beginning. How can evolutionists maintain that the universe evolved itself out of nothing? Creationists at least propose an adequate Cause to the beginning of the universe. For those who believe in God, creation is very reasonable.

In Jonathan Park & the Disaster at Brenan Bluff, Jonathan learned a lesson about his pride. Do you remember the verse his mother Angela shared?

"Pride goeth before destruction, and an haughty spirit before a fall." Proverbs 16:18

Usually when we are prideful, it's because we're trying to build ourselves up; but we need to remember that we're already someone special – we're the children of the Creator. When we build ourselves up, our attention is on us, not on God!

39

Do fossils prove Evolution?

Just like there're two
sides to every coin...

...there're two sides to the
evolution/creation debate!

Evolution

Evolution teaches that living things
started out as single-celled
organisms in the ocean, changed
over millions of years into fish,
and then crawled out on land.
Then, over millions of years, life
turned into thousands of different
animals, one of which was an ape-
like creature. This creature then
finally evolved into humans.

Creation

Creation says that an intelligent
Creator made plants, animals, and
people fully formed from the very
beginning – one type of animal
didn't change into another.
Although there were distinct kinds
of animals, God created them with
the ability to adapt and vary within
their specific kind. Therefore, the
changes in a kind of animal would
be limited and changes from one
kind to another would be impossible..

If there're two different views, how do we know which one is right?

When we find fossils, they tell the story of animals that once lived. This fossil history is known as the fossil record. The evidence from this record should help us discover the truth!

Evolution

Creation

Evolutionists believe the fossil record is the history of millions of years of evolution. They often use charts like the one to the right to illustrate their belief about the fossil record. If evolution is true, there should be two things we find in the fossil record:

Simple fossils should be found toward the beginning of time (at the bottom of the chart) and they should become more complicated as they evolve upward.

We should be able to find transitional fossils – fossils that are half of one type of animal and half of something else.

If creation is true, the chart to the left tells a different story. Instead of millions of years of evolution, it would be thousands of animals buried during the same flood layer by layer. If creation is true, there should be two things we find in the fossil record:

Fossils in the fossil record are found in order by the order of their burial – from sea creatures at the bottom to land creatures at the top. Complexity would be present at every level.

Instead of finding transitional fossils, we should find fossils of animals that are fully formed and look similar to the same animals we see today.

Instead of showing a perfect evolutionary transition from simple to complex, the fossil record reveals complex animals at all levels. As a matter of fact, some groups of animals – like mollusks who live in shells – are found at the top as well as at the bottom. Mammals and dinosaurs are found together. Think of the evolutionary "ages" as ecosystems – all buried sequentially by advancing flood waters. Groups and kinds of animals, like bony fish, appear abruptly in the fossil record and don't show evidence of changing into completely different types of animals. Since we've found millions of fossils, we should also find hundreds of thousands of transitional fossils (which show one animal turning into another) – yet we haven't. Instead, the fossil record contains fossils very similar to animals we see alive today! This evidence seems to disprove evolution and is excellent proof for creation!

The theory of Evolution teaches that **"Survival of the Fittest"** allows a newly evolved animal to live, while the unfit animals die out. However, just think about the idea that dinosaurs evolved into birds. Now remember evolution doesn't happen at all, but let's pretend that it could for just a moment. Can you imagine what would happen to the poor dinosaur's arms when they were halfway to evolving into wings? He would no longer be able to use his arms for eating and fighting, but he wouldn't be able to fly either – they'd be useless! How long do you think he'd last like that? That's just another reason why the evolutionary story can't be true, and why we don't find transitional fossils!

42

Evolutionists claim that "ape-man" fossils prove evolution, but the evidence shows something else!

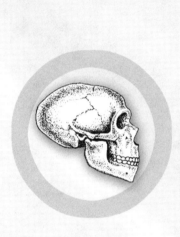

Neanderthals

For the most part, Neanderthal skulls we've found have had slightly bigger cranial capacity than the average person – but no different from some people alive today. Although many evolutionary scientists claim Neanderthals were an evolutionary break-away from human ancestry, many other scientists now agree that Neanderthals were fully human. We've even found evidence that Neanderthals created musical instruments, made tools, buried their dead, and had religious traditions just like modern humans. Yet, most of the public has only seen pictures of the Neanderthal people as ape-like brutes – cave men.

Cro-Magnon

Complete skeletons of the Cro-Magnon Man have been found. Their cranial capacity was about the same as modern man's. If Cro-Magnon were alive today and walking down the street in a business suit, he would go completely unnoticed.

Ramapithecus

Over 60 years ago, part of a fossilized jaw and a few teeth were discovered in India. Some declared that these fossils proved this creature was on its way to becoming man and that it walked upright, like humans. However, more fossils have been recovered, and the experts now admit that Ramapithecus was just an orangutan.

Lucy

Ever since she was found in 1973, "Lucy" has been one of the favorite "ape-man" fossils used by evolutionists.

In truth, Lucy is very similar to modern-day chimps. What got evolutionists excited about Lucy was that she seemed to have a hip joint that would allow her to walk more upright than most chimps. For evolutionists, this was excellent proof she was evolving into a human. The problem, however, is that even modern-day chimpanzees can walk upright for short periods of time. Also, Lucy had a "U" shaped jaw – typical of a chimp – and long curved toes and fingers that indicate she spent most of her time in the trees. Instead of saying Lucy was our evolutionary ancestor, the evidence better fits with the theory that Lucy was simply a type of chimpanzee that became extinct.

How to convince people that "ape-men" are real...

Oftentimes when a new fossil is discovered, an artist will make a drawing based on the few fragments of fossil that have been found.

When they find a fossil that is an ape, they try to make it look more human-like. When they discover a human fossil, they try to make it look more ape-like.

By using these types of artist's drawings, many people will become easily convinced that a new fossil is really half-man, half-ape.

The previous pages are just a few discoveries of the fossils that evolutionists claim as fossil evidence for the evolution of man. There are more, but they all fall into two categories:

1. **Within the range of modern human characteristics.**

2. **Similar to modern apes.**

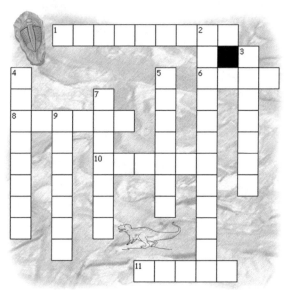

Fossil Crossword

Across

1. So-called ape-man fossils are never found in one complete skeleton, but usually in small _____.

6. Evolutionists believe we evolved from _____.

8. We can find out about fossils in the fossil _____.

10. Pictures of ape-man are usually drawn by an _____, not by a scientist.

11. Book that tells the truth about our beginning.

Down

2. If animals turned into other types of animals over millions of years, we should find _____ fossils.

3. Book in the Bible that tells how we were created.

4. Even if evolution could happen, "_____ of the fittest" would kill off animals like a dinosaur whose arm is half-way between an arm and a wing.

5. Bones that have turned to stones.

7. The One who made everything.

9. The fossil record doesn't show that animals evolved from simple to _____.

Could There Be Intelligent Life Out There?

**If evolution happened on Earth,
couldn't life have evolved on other planets as well?**

is Evolution Even Possible?

The Mathematical Odds are Against Evolution!

How many ways can two people stand in line?

To get the answer, we can use the equation:

1 x 2 = 2

**Two
Possibilities**

| The woman is on the left, the man on the right. | The man is on the left, the woman on the right. |

How many ways can three people stand in line?

1 x 2 x 3 = 6

A   **B**   **C**

Three people can stand in line six different ways!

1. A, B, C   4. B, C, A
2. A, C, B   5. C, A, B
3. B, A, C   6. C, B, A

How many ways can *eighteen* people stand in line?

**1x2x3x4x5x6x7x8x9x10x11x12x13x14x15x16x17x18
=6,402,373,705,728,000**

Over Six Quadrillion Possibilities!

If 18 people could switch places in line once every minute, it would take them over 12 billion years to stand in every possible order in line!

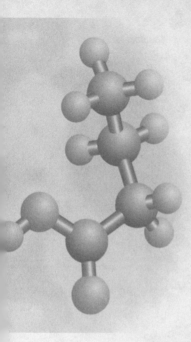

Many evolutionists now believe that the universe is around 12 billion years old (even though science shows it to be much younger). This would mean that if 18 people could switch places every minute through the entire course of evolutionary history, there wouldn't be enough time for them to line up in all the different possible ways!

Bad News for Evolution.

It takes an average of 400 amino acids to make up one protein in our body – they have to line up in perfect order. It also takes 60,000 proteins to make up a cell. Even more, our bodies are made from trillions of cells. If 18 people can't even line up in all the possible ways in 12 billion years, random evolution couldn't have lined up all the ingredients necessary to make our super complex human bodies!

Some evolutionists have realized that the mathematical odds are against evolution here on planet Earth. To solve their problem, they've come up with a new idea – that aliens brought life to earth and dropped it off in the ocean! Maybe we were a science project by alien beings! Maybe that would explain where life came from!

However, they still haven't solved the problem – in fact they've made it even worse. If evolution can't create life on planet Earth, how could it do it anywhere else either – how could evolution make aliens in the first place? Whoops, they're back to the same problem; evolution can't create life, only God can!

After many years of searching, we still haven't found any evidence for extraterrestrial life!

Listening to the Airwaves

If intelligent life really exists somewhere else in the universe, wouldn't they have radio and TV signals similar to ours? It was this idea that drove Frank Drake in the fall of 1960 to begin listening for radio signals from space. He called it Project Ozma. Since that time there've been many others, including SETI (Search for ExtraTerrestrial Intelligence) and Project Phoenix. Today there are about a dozen other major radio telescopes listening to the skies!

Although there have been some false alarms, in over four decades, mankind has never detected an intelligent signal coming from anywhere other than planet Earth! It seems that our radio telescopes are telling us we are alone in the universe.

If there are no aliens, what are UFOs?

UFO stands for Unidentified Flying Object, and many times that's just what they are – unidentified objects. People may see some type of natural phenomenon that looks very strange. Many times people are so set on seeing a UFO that they interpret what they see as a UFO. Also, many tricks have occurred where someone faked a spaceship. However, there are some sightings difficult to explain away. Some have speculated that these may be a spiritual deception.

Although scientists haven't detected radio signals from space, there are many other ways mankind has looked for intelligent life in our galaxy. In 1976, NASA launched two probes, Viking I and Viking II. These spacecraft mapped the surface of Mars and searched for signs of life. Since that time, NASA has spent billions of dollars looking for life throughout our universe – this includes the recent wave of probes to Mars over the past several years. So far, there hasn't been any evidence at all that there is intelligent life anywhere but here on Earth.

Lately, many scientists have begun looking for water on other planets. Since water is necessary for life, they think that if they find water on a planet then life might have evolved there. However, this is a silly idea – first of all life doesn't evolve; and secondly, life needs so much more than water – life is a special creation by God!

Couldn't God have created life on other planets?

Many Christians ask this question: If intelligent life exists on other planets, maybe God created it? At first this sounds good, but there are many problems with this idea. Here are just a few:

In Romans 8:22, the Bible says that the whole creation was cursed because of our sin. If that is true, would God punish other alien civilizations because of our sin? That doesn't sound like a just and loving God. Another possibility is that all alien civilizations sinned at exactly the same instant as Adam and Eve, but that seems pretty impossible. And further, would Jesus have to go from planet to planet dying for each alien people? No, that can't be, because in Hebrews 10:10 it says, "...we are sanctified through the offering of the body of Jesus Christ once for all." You see, if we believe that God created aliens living on other planets, it really makes things in the Bible become very strange. So why stretch God's Word to include aliens, when there isn't any proof that they exist in the first place?

In *Jonathan Park & the Escape from Utopia*, Katie learned an important lesson about trusting God's Word. When she saw the UFO with her own eyes, it made her doubt the Bible. But remember the verse she learned?

"Sanctify them through thy truth: thy word is truth." - *John 17:17.*

After she learned the UFO wasn't real, she realized she could always trust God's Word!

Earth is designed especially for life!

Evolutionists love to point out that with all of the star systems and planets, the universe has to be teeming with life. Do you know how many planets have been found that can support life? Is it...
a. 0   b. 1   c. 25   d. 100

The correct answer is "b". There's only one planet that can support life – Earth. Here are some interesting facts about how the Creator made Earth special:

•If Earth were a tiny bit closer to the sun, we'd be fried; but if we were much further away, we'd freeze to death.

•The amount of oxygen in our air is just right. If there were a little less, we wouldn't be able to breathe; if there were more, Earth would burst into flames!

•Our atmosphere protects us from deadly rays of the sun while letting in the light and energy we need.

•The water cycle gives us a constant life-giving water supply.

When Tadpoles Change into Frogs, Doesn't that Prove Evolution?

Tadpoles are much different from the frogs they'll soon become. They have no jaws, lungs, or eyelids; and their skeleton is made of cartilage. During their growth, they begin to change – the tail is lost and limbs appear. The first changes to appear are 'buds', which later grow into the frog's hind legs. Soon the front legs grow, and the tail begins to shrink as the body absorbs it. Next, jaws and teeth develop. Cartilage turns into hardened bone, and the long, coiled intestine of the tadpole shrinks to the short intestine of the adult.

The tadpole's ability to change is already pre-programmed into its genes. This is just another amazing example of how wonderfully the Creator made the animals. How creative that God made the tadpole travel such a fascinating journey to becoming an adult frog!

Many people try to point to this incredible change in the tadpole, as an example of evolution. But that's not evolution at all. Evolution means that an animal kind gradually changes into a completely different kind of animal over long periods of time because of mistakes in their genes that add new information. However, this has never been observed.

Like the frog, the chameleon lizard also has an amazing ability – it can change color! Under the skin of this lizard is a layer of cells that contains red and yellow pigments. Below that layer are more cells that reflect white and blue light. Even deeper is a layer of brown melanin – another pigment. Using these special cells beneath its skin, a chameleon can turn blue, green, yellow, red, black, white, and brown. Although many believe a chameleon changes colors because of the surrounding colors, it's actually influenced by its mood, the surrounding light, and temperature. However, these factors are controlled by the environment and usually do turn the lizard the same color as the surroundings nearby.

Sadly, many evolutionists say that such a fantastic creature just accidentally evolved by random chance – but the evidence really points to the truth that the Creator designed them. He gave them this ability as a way to hide from another animals that may harm them. Only God can program into the genes of the chameleon the ability to change color!

Macro- vs. Micro Evolution

Many people don't realize that two very different ideas are called evolution. When people say "evolution," most of the time they really mean macroevolution. Macroevolution is the belief that one animal kind can gradually turn into another animal kind over millions of years by mistakes called mutations. How could many mistakes add new information to the genetic code and thereby make a new animal?

The term microevolution most often refers to adaptation and variation within the same kind of animal. Unlike macroevolution, microevolution includes changes that are already programmed into an animal's genes. For example, only two of the dog kind – one male and one female – (probably most like today's wolves) got on board Noah's Ark. From that pair, we now have wolves, coyotes, domestic dogs, and many other wild dogs. Microevolution is a proven fact of science, and it is completely different from macroevolution.

Does Australia really exist?

At first this may sound like an odd question, but if you've never been to Australia, how do you know that it's really there?

Most of us have never seen Australia, so we have to accept the evidence that it exists...

We can read about Australia in history and geography books. The facts that we read fit with other information that we've received about Australia.

People can tell us about their personal experiences visiting Australia. These testimonies are consistent with other people's stories about that country.

We've seen actual pictures of Australia. These pictures are observable evidence that Australia really does exist. However, we must have faith that the author, traveler, or photographer is honest and accurate.

If God really does exist, there should be evidence that He is really there...

We can read about the Creator in the history written down in the Bible. The kings, people, and places we read about in God's Word are often confirmed by archaeological discoveries!

People who lived during Biblical times have written about their firsthand experience with God. These accounts are consistent with other written testimonies.

When God created the world, He left behind evidence of what He did. There's design in every animal, geologic evidence of Noah's Flood, and much more. This scientific evidence is observable evidence that He does exist!

WORD SCRAMBLE

Clues

1. This scientific theory has never been proven by science.

2. The blueprints for life are stored here.

3. During the week of creation, God created each _____ of animal.

4. According to evolution, a single-celled organism changed into all kinds of animals through _____ changes over millions of years.

5. Evolution claims everything in the universe came about by _____.

6. The Bible tells us everything in the universe came about by God's ____.

7. God designed the _____ lizard to change color.

8. When people say the word "evolution" they usually mean ___ evolution.

9. Examples of "evolution" are always ___ evolution (adaptation).

10. Animals can adapt because God _____ this ability into their genes.

11. Christianity isn't a blind faith, but in harmony with scientific _____.

12. The _____ seal from Nineveh may support the Genesis account.

13. The Garden of _____.

14. There's lots of scientific evidence that God does _____.

Copy the letters in the numbered squares above to the

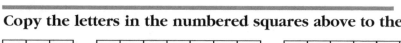

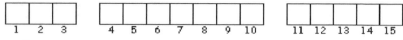

Scrambled Words

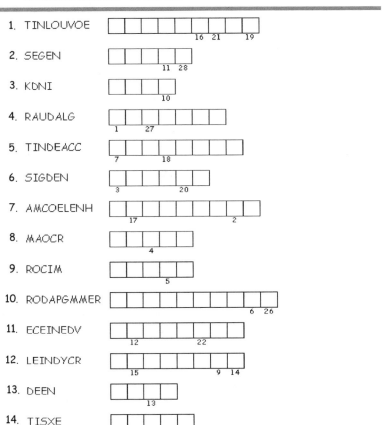

1. TINLOUVOE [ ][ ][ ][ ][ ][ ][ ][ ][ ]
   _16_ _21_ _19_

2. SEGEN [ ][ ][ ][ ][ ]
   _11_ _28_

3. KDNI [ ][ ][ ][ ]
   _10_

4. RAUDALG [ ][ ][ ][ ][ ][ ][ ]
   _1_ _27_

5. TINDEACC [ ][ ][ ][ ][ ][ ][ ][ ]
   _7_   _18_

6. SIGDEN [ ][ ][ ][ ][ ][ ]
   _3_   _20_

7. AMCOELENH [ ][ ][ ][ ][ ][ ][ ][ ][ ]
   _17_   _2_

8. MAOCR [ ][ ][ ][ ][ ]
   _4_

9. ROCIM [ ][ ][ ][ ][ ]
   _5_

10. RODAPGMMER [ ][ ][ ][ ][ ][ ][ ][ ][ ][ ]
    _6_ _26_

11. ECEINEDV [ ][ ][ ][ ][ ][ ][ ][ ]
    _12_   _22_

12. LEINDYCR [ ][ ][ ][ ][ ][ ][ ][ ]
    _15_   _9_ _14_

13. DEEN [ ][ ][ ][ ]
    _13_

14. TISXE [ ][ ][ ][ ][ ]
    _25_ _24_ _23_ _8_

squares below to learn the hidden message.

[ ][ ][ ][ ]   [ ][ ]   [ ][ ][ ]   [ ][ ][ ][ ].
_17_ _18_ _19_ _20_   _21_ _22_   _23_ _24_ _25_   _26_ _27_ _15_ _28_

59

... there's evidence that the
"Garden of Eden" really existed?

In the British Museum, there's an ancient cylinder seal on display, rediscovered from the ancient civilization of Nineveh. Long ago, seals like this were used to record history. When this cylinder is rolled across soft clay, it forms a picture. In the center of this picture stands a tree. To the right of the tree is a man, to the left a woman. It appears that the woman is picking fruit from the tree. A snake stretches up behind her. This seal seems to be telling the story of the Garden of Eden.

If the Bible is true, then all people descended from Adam and Eve. The history of these events would be handed down. Story tellers might have changed some of the details, but the basic story would remain the same. That's the exciting thing about this cylinder – it's dated between 2200 and 2100 BC, possibly around the time of Abraham. While the Old Testament tells the story of Eden, this seal came from another people group that tells the same story!

In *Jonathan Park and the Clue from Nineveh*, Jonathan and Rusty were pestering each other. Rusty isn't a Christian, and Jonathan should've known better. For a Christian, when someone wrongs us, we should pay back evil with kindness. Do you remember the verse that Jonathan's dad, Kendall, brought to memory? It was Matthew 5:44,

"But I say unto you, Love your enemies, bless them that curse you, do good to them that hate you, and pray for them which despitefully use you, and persecute you;"

As Christians, we're supposed to be the ones to set the example. Are you willing to love your enemies and pray for those who persecute you?

Fibonacci Numbers make patterns we see everywhere!

Each number in the sequence can be calculated by adding the last two numbers together!

0-1-1-2-3-5-8-13-21-34-55-89

3+5=8

21+34=55

What comes after 89?

To find out, we add 89 to the number before it: $55 + 89 = 144$

Can you calculate the next two numbers?

$$55 - 89 - 144 - \underline{} - \underline{}$$

Answer: 233 - 377

61

A great example is found in the seeds of a sunflower.

If you look at the head of a sunflower, you'll notice that the seeds are arranged in two spiral patterns. If you count the seeds in a smaller sunflower, the seeds will oftentimes have 34 in one spiral and 55 in the other. A larger sunflower will usually have 55 in one direction and 89 in the other. You'll notice that these numbers are found in the Fibonacci number sequence.

Sunflowers are just one example. You will find similar patterns in the seeds of a daisy. Numbers in the Fibonacci sequence are found even in the patterns of pinecones.

The Golden Rectangle

Fibonacci numbers can also make the shape known as the **Golden Rectangle**. These special rectangles are formed by using two consecutive numbers from the Fibonacci sequence for the length and width.

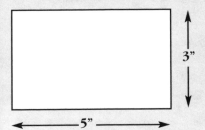

A great example is 3 x 5 note card. Since its height and width are made from numbers that are found together in the Fibonacci sequence, it is a **golden rectangle**.

Using any two consecutive Fibonacci numbers, and a ruler, can you draw your own golden rectangle in the space below?

Where did the word, "Fibonacci" come from?

The word "Fibonacci" may sound like the name of a pizza restaurant, but it was actually the nickname for a man whose real name was Leonardo Pisa. Since Leonardo Pisa is the one who discovered the Fibonacci sequence, everyone began calling them Fibonacci numbers.

It was back in the medieval times that Fibonacci discovered these marvelous numbers while studying rabbits. He used an ideal situation in which one pair of rabbits over a period of seven months multiplies to become 13 pairs of rabbits.

Find a book on Fibonacci and his numbers. Maybe you will find the diagram that shows exactly how one pair of rabbits becomes 13 pairs. Need a clue? A lot of Fibonacci numbers will be found between the first pair and the 13 pairs seven months later.

That's how it all began!

0-1-1-2-3-5-8-13-21-34-55-89

The Golden Ratio

A ratio is a number that shows the relationship between two other numbers.

For example, we can show the relationship between the height and width of a

rectangle. To do this, we can divide the height by the width. On this 3 x 5

card we can divide 3 by 5 to get the ratio of the height to width: $3 \div 5 = .6$

Likewise, we can divide the width by the height: $5 \div 3 = 1.66666$

The ratios for every single Golden Rectangle will turn out as .6 or 1.6 *(when*

we ignore digits to the right of the tenth's place.)

Try to calculate the ratios for the rectangle that you drew on the other side of

this sheet. Does it come out to .6 or 1.6?

God, the Artist

Fibonacci patterns are found throughout the universe, and they add beauty to our planet. If our world really were the result of a big-bang random chance, we shouldn't find any of these patterns.

Instead, it appears that the Creator has made things beautiful – like a divine artist. Fibonacci patterns are just a reminder of His creativity!

Since Fibonacci patterns are so beautiful, many human artists have used them in their own works – artists like: Leonardo de Vinci, Van Gogh, Vermeer, Monet, and many others.

The Golden Spiral

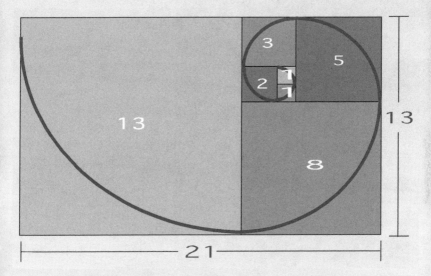

Another fascinating shape that can be made from Fibonnaci numbers is the **Golden Spiral**. Notice that the above rectangle is a **Golden Rectangle** – the lengths of its sides are made from two consecutive numbers in the Fibonacci sequence: 13 & 21. Next we divide the rectangle into smaller boxes in a pattern, as in the picture above. See how the sizes of the boxes are in order of the Fibonacci series: 1, 1, 2, 3, 5, 8, and 13? By drawing a curve that swirls through each square, the result is the golden spiral!

Fibonacci patterns are also in you! They're found in the sections of your fingers, on the features of your face, and even throughout your entire body. It's just another reminder that you didn't happen by chance, but the Creator specially made you!

"For thou hast possessed my reins: thou hast covered me in my mother's womb. I will praise thee; for I am fearfully and wonderfully made: marvellous are thy works; and that my soul knoweth right well. My substance was not hid from thee, when I was made in secret, and curiously wrought in the lowest parts of the earth."

— Psalm 139:13-15

What is Information?

Information is a message that has meaning.

If you accidentally spilled ink on a piece of paper, would that be information?
Not really.

Woops! The printer must've blobbed this ink right here onto the paper!

Would there be information if you used that same ink and arranged it into letters on the same piece of paper? Yes.

Which makes more sense to you? Is it the blob above or this message?

How interesting. Even though we used the same paper and ink, we now have a message. That tells us something very important about information…

Information is separate from the object that holds it!

In some ways, you could think of information like water. A cup can hold water, but water really isn't part of the cup.

Objects hold information, too. When you write a message on a piece of paper, you're actually storing information in paper and ink.

Just like pouring water into another glass, information can be transferred from one object to another. For example, you can transfer information from one sheet of paper to another by making a photocopy.

Information is separate from objects, but can be stored and passed on by them.

Information can be...
...placed on the pages of a book.

...stored on a CD-ROM.

...displayed on the LCD of a calculator.

...sent by e-mail.

...broadcast through the air on radio waves.

...transmitted by flashing a Morse code message through a ship's signal light.

Since information is separate from material objects, that means that information isn't like an object at all. And since information isn't an object, that means non-thinking things cannot make that information. Instead, information always comes from an intelligent, thinking source – like a person!

The **Safe**

Pretend that you locked a blank sheet of paper in a safe and that only you had the combination. If you returned in a hundred years (wow, you'd really be old!) and unlocked the safe, what would you expect to find on the paper? How about a message that said, "This message just appeared by random chance on this piece of paper!" NO! That would be ridiculous! That's because information can come only from an intelligent (thinking) source – like a person. No matter how long you left that paper in the safe, it would remain blank.

However, what would it mean if you opened the safe one day and you found a message written on the paper, which at the bottom was signed by Fred? Since a message couldn't write itself, you would assume that someone had found the combination to the safe and wrote you a message. Furthermore, that writer was someone named Fred.

It's the same thing with our universe – there's a vast amount of information everywhere. It's like a message, and it was signed by the Creator!

Hello,
I just wanted to let you know I found out the combination to the safe and decided to write you this message.
Fred

Problem for Evolution

The Theory of Evolution says that the entire universe was created by a "Big Bang" – that a huge explosion began the evolution of all its objects. Even so, if all that ever existed were material objects, where did information come from? Remember that non-thinking objects can't make anything. Saying that the "Big Bang" could create all the information that we see in the world would be as silly as saying that a CD-ROM made up its own program!

Einstein's Gulf

Albert Einstein said there's a big difference between objects and words about objects.

For example...

A car is a real object.

A car can never turn itself into words about itself.

Unbridgeable

Gulf

To get across you need intelligence.

But *words* about a car are something totally different...

Words about a car can never turn themselves into a real car.

"We have the habit of combining certain concepts and conceptual relations (propositions) so definitely with certain sense experiences that we do not become conscious of the gulf—logically unbridgeable—which separates the world of sensory experiences from the world of concepts and propositions."

English Translation:

Basically, what Einstein was saying is that words become so real to us that we forget that they aren't really the object itself. He says that, in fact, words and objects are so different that there is a huge gulf – or gap – between them. In other words, words (or information) are separate from objects.

Remember our cup and water? Information is separate from objects.

So, words are simply information that can represent objects.

A blueprint is information about a house.

Blueprints
Jones House

Acme
Construction

A blueprint could never turn itself into a house, and a house could never design its own blueprint.

Can a house draw its own blueprint? No, of course not! The "logically unbridgeable gulf" to which Albert Einstein was referring cannot be crossed without intelligence.

But with intelligence it can be done! For instance, an architect can use his intelligence to produce blueprints; and, with the right materials and some work, a builder can turn the blueprints into a house.

So, Einstein's Gulf Can Be Crossed, But Only With Intelligence!

Like a blueprint for a house, each living thing has a blueprint known as the genetic code. This information is what your body needs to make you unique – the kind of hair you have, the color of your eyes, how tall you'll be, etc. This code uses a language made up from its own very special words.

More Big Problems for Evolution

According to evolutionary theory, all that existed at the start were non-living objects. Then after a very long time, the genetic code accidentally came into being. Living creatures just arranged themselves according to elaborate plans written in DNA, all by accident. Evolutionary theory claims that objects crossed Einstein's Gulf without any intelligence at all! According to Einstein, that's impossible! Remember that an object can't make words that describe itself. Just like a car can't make words about itself, living creatures could not have created the original language found in their own genetic code!

75

So, the Theory of evolution can't be true because it is contrary to Einstein's Gulf. But remember, it has even larger problems than that! How could random chance accidents create life or the genetic code in the first place?

EVOLUTION or CREATION?

Information is excellent proof that the Creator made both the living creatures and the genetic code – He's the intelligence that crosses Einstein's Gulf.

Tons of Information

The amount of information in your DNA alone is amazing. It would fill more than an entire set of encyclopedias! However, if you consider the information – not only in your DNA but also in your brain and the rest of your body – all the books in a library with over 10,000 books wouldn't be able to hold all of that information!

Now consider all the billions of people and animals living on earth – what an amazing amount of information! God is truly a magnificent Creator – His creativity is beyond our understanding!

Charles Darwin

Charles Darwin
1809 - 1882

Although evolutionary ideas have been around for thousands of years, Charles Darwin is often credited for inventing the modern theory of evolution. He is most famous for his book, "The Origin of Species." Even though Darwin loved science, his only official training was to prepare him for the ministry. He studied at Christ's College in Cambridge, England.

Sadly, Charles Darwin lost faith in God's Word. While there were many factors that influenced his unbelief, one of the most powerful was "the problem of evil." He could not understand why a good and loving God would allow death, pain, and suffering.

The Problem of Evil

If God is so good and loving, why does He allow death, pain, and suffering?

Like Charles Darwin, many skeptics ask this question – and it's an important one to ask. Why does God allow evil?

However, when people ask this question, they're forgetting one very important thing – God created the world perfect...

"And God saw every thing that he had made, and, behold, it was very good. And the evening and the morning were the sixth day." – Genesis 1:31

The reason there's death, pain, and suffering in the world is that mankind rebelled against God...

"Wherefore, as by one man sin entered into the world, and death by sin; and so death passed upon all men, for that all have sinned." – Romans 5:12

So you see, it isn't God's fault that there's death, pain, and suffering in the world. It was our fault. We disobeyed God, and He allowed consequences. Think about it: Many of the evil things that happen to us are a result of our own wicked heart. However, the Creator loved us so much that He didn't leave it there...

"But God commendeth his love toward us, in that, while we were yet sinners, Christ died for us." – Romans 5:7

Death, pain, and suffering will someday be gone because of what Jesus did for us on the cross!

"And God shall wipe away all tears from their eyes; and there shall be no more death, neither sorrow, nor crying, neither shall there be any more pain: for the former things are passed away." – Revelation 21:4

One of Darwin's favorite books was "Principles of Geology" by Charles Lyell. Before Lyell published his book, most people thought that a great worldwide flood formed the huge rock layers found around the earth.

However, Charles Lyell proposed that these rock layers were actually deposited very, very slowly over millions of years. In his book, he ridiculed belief in a young creation and taught that the earth was very old.

1- The Voyage

On December 27, 1831, Darwin boarded a ship named the HMS Beagle. They sailed from Plymouth Harbor, England to the Santa Cruz River Valley in Argentina.

When they arrived, Darwin looked at the small river that wound its way through the huge valley. After reading Lyell's book, Darwin wondered if it were possible that this little river carved out the canyon over millions of years. It made sense to him.

It was here at the Santa Cruz River Valley that Darwin really accepted geological gradualism – the idea that geologic formations take millions of years to form.

2- On to the Galapagos Islands

After the Santa Cruz River, the Beagle continued on its way to the Galapagos Islands.

Darwin observed the finches that lived there. He collected some and sent them back to a man in England who studied them and divided them into 13 different species. The man noticed some of these finches had long beaks and others had shorter ones.

When Darwin returned home, he began to wonder if the finches were changing slowly over time. He remembered the observations about the river valley being carved very slowly. That's when he took the idea of geological gradualism and made a new theory – biological gradualism, the idea that one type of animal can slowly change into another. That was the birth of the modern-day theory of evolution.

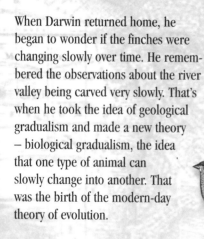

Darwin's Wrong Turn

The sad thing about Darwin's voyage is that he took a wrong turn at the Santa Cruz River Valley – a wrong turn in his thinking. Darwin was wrong about the Santa Cruz River!

Almost all geologists now agree that the Santa Cruz River Valley was not formed by the river over millions of years. Instead, there's much evidence that the river was carved out when a large glacial lake in the mountains above the valley broke through a natural glacial dam, producing large amounts of water that created the Santa Cruz Valley in a very short time.

That's the funny thing about that canyon – it was the foundation for Darwin's belief in geological gradualism and millions of years – but he was wrong! It was also the basis for his belief that animals could gradually evolve. So, if Darwin was wrong about the Santa Cruz Valley, could he also be wrong about his theory of evolution?

Are the finches at the Galapagos Islands changing?

Yes, they are!

So does that mean that evolution is true?

No!

Many people don't realize that there are
two types of evolution…

1. Macroevolution

2. Microevolution

Since the time of Darwin, many scientists have been observing the finches living
on the Galapagos Islands. It is true that their beaks are different lengths and that
these birds have different coloring.

Animals have a blueprint for life.
This plan is contained in the genetic
code. According to evolutionists,
random mistakes that happen in this
code can change an animal for the
better. But think about it: If you took
a blueprint for a building, and
added a mistake, would it make the
building better or worse? Of course
it would be worse – that's why it's
called a mistake!

Macroevolution

This idea is what people normally call the theory of evolution.

Macroevolution...

- means that one type of animal changes into another type over a very long time.

- happens because of mistakes (mutations) in a creature's genetic code.

- would need thousands of good mutations that would make an animal type better and better.

Microevolution

This idea is what people normally call adaptation and variation.

Microevolution...

- means that a type of animal may have several different varieties but will not become a completely different type of creature.

- is a change that is already programmed into an animal's genetic code.

- sometimes allows animals to adapt to their environment.

While it is true that the finches on the Galapagos Islands are changing, they aren't gradually evolving into other types of animals. Instead, they're varying according to the possibilities already programmed into their genetic code. To be evidence for macro-evolution, these birds should be changing into another animal or type of bird – but they're still birds and they are still finches!

Dogs, Dogs, DOGS

Dogs are an excellent example of variation. Think of all the different varieties of dogs... big ones, small ones, cute ones, and ugly ones.

All of these varieties of dogs were bred from an original dog kind. Programmed into these dogs was the information necessary to produce all the modern varieties we see today – but no one has ever seen a dog change slowly into anything other than a dog!

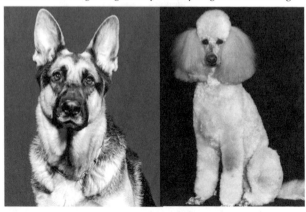

A Pair of Dice Explains the Difference

Between Microevolution & Macroevolution.

Microevolution

Just think about it: with two dice, you can roll any number between 2 and 12.

That would be like microevolution. Each time you roll the dice, there would be a variety of possible numbers that could come up. There are many different possibilities, but they are limited to what is already on the dice.

Likewise, that's how it is with adaptation and variation (microevolution). There are many different possible traits and varieties of a type of animal, but they are limited to what was already programmed into its genetic code.

Macroevolution

Macroevolution is like rolling the dice long enough that the edges would eventually wear off and the dice would slowly turn into checkers! That's as silly as saying that mistakes in an animal's genetic code can gradually turn one type of animal into a completely different type!

So, microevolution is adaptation and variation, and it is proven by science. Macroevolution is what is known as the theory of evolution, and it has never been observed!

Another great

example of variation is the

TASSEL-EARED SQUIRREL.

One animal that lives at the Grand Canyon is the Tassel-eared Squirrel. These squirrels are divided into two groups. On the north side of the canyon are the Kaibab Squirrels. Most of them have black stomachs and white tails.

On the south side of the canyon live the Abert Squirrels, with predominately white stomachs and black tails – just the opposite of the Kaibab squirrels. These two squirrels are exactly the same, except for the different colors on their coats.

The interesting thing is that after the Grand Canyon was formed, these two squirrels could never mix. The canyon is way too big for them to get across, much of the canyon is desert, and the river is too broad and powerful. The squirrel populations have been separated since the canyon was formed. So, since they can no longer mix, they have different physical traits, represented in each group.

Evolutionists would point out that these squirrels are evolving differently from one another, but there's a better explanation. The squirrels are actually good examples of limited change within a kind, not evolution. These color differences are an excellent example of variations already programmed in the squirrels' genetic code!

Another Type of Microevolution –

So far we've learned about adaptation and variation, but there's a different kind of microevolution...

Maybe you've heard of the blind cavefish? It lives in Texas, Mexico, and Central America, and all the way down into Panama. This fish doesn't have functioning eyes, but it's very similar to another fish that lives outside the cave. These two fish were probably the same until the cavefish lost its working eyes. What caused that to happen? Was it adaptation and variation? No, there's a better explanation. It's more likely that the change happened due to missing information, information included by the fishes' genes to build the eyes. Wait a minute: Doesn't that sound like evolution? Remember how we've learned that microevolution is the theory that animals can change from one type of animal into another type because of mistakes in their genetic code? So does this cavefish prove evolution? Not at all!

Mutations

When a mistake happens in an animal's genetic code, it can lose information. It's like a blueprint for a building. If you took those plans and randomly changed part of the information, the builders wouldn't know how to build that part of the structure. It would ruin the building! It's the same for the cavefish. Most likely, a genetic change modified the information needed to build the eyes for those fish; and so they developed without having any. Every time a mutation happens, information may be lost or corrupted!

Why are There Mutations?

If mutations are mistakes in the genetic code, why would God have allowed them? Well, actually God made the world perfect; but as a result of mankind's sin, the Creator allowed the consequences of our rebellion to ruin the world. Things are no longer perfect. Things wear out and die, and even mutations occur.

Evolution is Completely Opposite

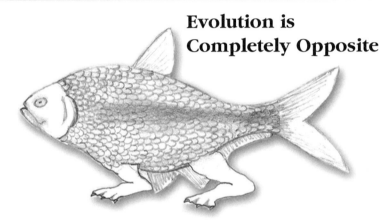

Let's pretend that these fish were going to evolve legs. Instead of losing information, as in the case of our cavefish, they would have to gain information to tell their bodies how to grow legs. However, that can't be true. Mutations may lose information – but they never supply new information, information which could produce novel, complex, working structures!

So one type of microevolution happens because information is lost. Macroevolution says that one type of animal can change into another because mistakes in its genes introduce new creative information instead of losing information – and that's never been proven by science!

The Media and Evolution

It's very common to hear in the media that someone has observed actual proof for evolution.

A great example of this is the finches at the Galapagos Islands. For many years, evolutionists have been watching those birds and publishing information showing that they're changing.

So what's the problem? Well, as you can guess, those evolutionists are finding excellent evidence for adaptation and variation (microevolution), but not for macroevolution.

This happens all the time in the media. They'll write a story about real proof for adaptation, but then at the end of the article, they'll call it evolution, even though it had nothing to do with evolution at all.

Sadly, many Christians are fooled by such reports. However, now that you know the difference, watch how they show adaptation and then say it proves the theory of evolution!

The Evidence is Everywhere!

"For the invisible things of him from the creation of the world are clearly seen, being understood by the things that are made, even his eternal power and Godhead; so that they are without excuse." – Romans 1:20

The evidence for the Creator is all around us – and especially when we look at the special ability God gave creatures to vary and adapt! There are so many animals, living in totally different environments all around the world, and they all have adapted to their unique environment. That shows how smart, creative, and loving our God is to make plants, animals, and us to live in this special world!

Getting into the Scriptures

A devotional for children & parents

1. Begin with Prayer!
2. Look up the Bible verses and fill in the blanks (Please note that the Scripture references listed are from the King James Version).
3. Parents, using the Scriptures in this study, take time to further explain the truths presented in each point.

Why is Creation Science So Important?

1 Evolution implies that there isn't a God who cares for you. Evolution supposedly takes place because of all the mistakes in our genetic code (the body's molecular system designed to transmit hereditary information). That means that all of us are here because of accidental mistakes. We have no purpose for our life. If there is a Creator God, then each of us is unique and there is a purpose and plan for our life.

Genesis 1:1, 26-27 - ¹*In the beginning God _____ the heaven and the earth…* ²⁶*And God said, Let us _____ man in our image, after our likeness: and let them have dominion over the fish of the sea, and over the fowl of the air, and over the cattle, and over all the earth, and over every creeping thing that creepeth upon the earth.* ²⁷*So God _____ man in his own image, in the image of God _____ he him; male and female _____ he them.*

Modern evolutionism claims that all life begins with elementary particles of matter evolving out of nothing from a "primordial soup" and then developing through natural forces into complex systems. However, very significantly, the concept of the special creation of the universe of space and time itself is found nowhere in all religion or philosophy, ancient or modern, except as it is in Genesis Chapter One.

Isaiah 45:5-6, 12 - ⁵*I am the LORD, and there is none else, there is no God beside me: I girded thee, though thou hast not known me:* ⁶*That they may know from the rising of the sun, and from the west, that there is none beside me. I am the LORD, and there is none else…* ¹²*I have _____ the earth, and _____ man upon it: I, even my hands, have stretched out the heavens, and all their host have I commanded.*

The Bible Reveals How Satan Tempted Adam and Eve to Disobey God, and this Resulted in Suffering and Death, and Separation from God.

Genesis 2:16-17 - *16And the LORD God commanded the man, saying, Of every tree of the garden thou mayest freely eat: 17But of the tree of the knowledge of good and evil, thou shalt not eat of it: for in the day that thou eatest thereof thou shalt surely _____.*

> The restriction imposed here by God is the simplest, most straightforward test that could be devised for determining man's voluntary response to God's love. There was only one minor restraint placed on Adam's freedom; and, with an abundance of delicious fruit of all types available, there was no justification for his desiring the one forbidden fruit. Nevertheless, he did have a choice, and so was a free moral agent, capable of accepting or rejecting God's will.

Romans 5:12 - *12Wherefore, as by one man sin entered into the world, and death _____ sin; and so death passed upon all men, for that all have sinned.*

> There was no death before sin entered the world. The finished creation was "very good" (Genesis 1:31). There was certainly no struggle for existence or survival of the fittest, for every creature was created fit for its own environment. When Adam sinned, God brought the curse of decay and death not only upon Adam but also upon all His dominion (Genesis 3:17-20; 1 Corinthians 15:21, 22; Romans 8:20-22).

In Romans 5:12 we see <u>the origin and power of death</u>. THE ORIGIN: "BY ONE MAN" – <u>Adam</u>. THE POWER: "PASSED UPON ALL MEN".

The Bible Reveals that Satan's Plan to Ruin Mankind was Overcome by the Salvation that God Provided for Fallen Man.

In Romans 5:15-19, we also see the origin of power over death. This too is "BY ONE MAN" – Jesus Christ. Its power is for "ALL MEN UNTO JUSTIFICATION." Therefore it could be stated that the world was changed forever by two historical figures (1 Corinthians 15:22, 45).

The "seed of the woman" can only be an allusion to a future descendant of Eve who would have no human father. Biologically, a woman produces no seed (except in this case, Biblical usage always speaks only of the seed of men). This promised Seed would, therefore, have to be miraculously implanted in the womb. In this way, He would not inherit the sin nature which would disqualify every son of Adam from becoming a Savior from sin. This prophecy thus clearly anticipates the future virgin birth of Christ.

The first prophecy of salvation through Jesus Christ is mentioned in *Genesis 3:14-15*. *14And the LORD God said unto the serpent, Because thou hast done this, thou art cursed above all cattle, and above every beast of the field; upon thy belly shalt thou go, and dust shalt thou eat all the days of thy life: 15And I will put enmity between thee and the woman, and between thy seed and her seed; – _____ shall bruise thy head, and thou shalt bruise _____ heel.*

The Bible Reveals that God Has Provided Forgiveness for Man's Sin By Grace Through Faith in Jesus Christ.

It is clear from the teaching in the Bible that none of us deserves to be forgiven – we all do wrong and terrible things. We all deserve the judgment which God has pronounced upon us.

Romans 6:23 - *23For the _____ of sin is death; but the gift of God is eternal life through Jesus Christ our Lord.*

John 3:18 - *18He that believeth on him is not condemned: but he that believeth not is condemned _____ , because he hath not believed in the name of the only begotten Son of God.*

God didn't leave it there. For the children of God, His forgiveness is nothing we deserve. Because God still loves fallen man, He wants to forgive us of all our sin.

1 Peter 3:18a - *18For Christ also hath once suffered for sins, the just for the _____, that he might bring us to God, being put to death in the flesh…*

Ephesians 2:8-9 - *8For by grace are ye saved through faith; and that not of _____: it is the gift of God: 9Not of _____, lest any man should boast.*

We all deserve to die and to be separated from God. Jesus took the death penalty that we deserve, so that we can be restored to God and spend eternity with Him.

When we realize that there is nothing we could do on our own, it's then that we will simply accept what Jesus Christ has already done.

John 3:16-17 - ¹⁶*For God so loved the world, that he _____ his only begotten Son, that whosoever believeth in him should not perish but have everlasting life.* ¹⁷*For God sent not his Son into the world to condemn the world; but that the world _____ him might be saved.*

By Faith You Must Accept Jesus Christ as Your Personal Savior and Lord as Your Only Hope of Heaven.

Romans 10:9-10, 13 - ⁹*That if thou shalt confess with thy mouth the Lord Jesus, and shalt believe in thine heart that God hath raised him from the dead, thou shalt be saved.* ¹⁰*For with the heart man believeth unto righteousness; and with the mouth confession is made unto salvation...*¹³*For whosoever _____ call upon the name of the Lord shall be saved.*

John 1:12 - ¹²*But as many as _____ him, to them gave he power to become the sons of God, even to them that believe on his name.*

According to the last two verses listed, if you call upon Jesus Christ to save you, and then you receive Christ by simply believing that He died for your sins, will God save you? Yes, He will!

Pray a prayer to God admitting that you are a sinner and cannot save yourself. Ask Jesus to save you and come into your heart.

Now read your Bible, find a Bible-believing church, and learn more about the real God who saves you.